Nature's Fury
TSUNAMIS

John Hamilton

ABDO
& Daughters

VISIT US AT

WWW.ABDOPUB.COM

Published by ABDO Publishing Company, 4940 Viking Drive, Suite 622, Edina, Minnesota 55435.
Copyright ©2006 by Abdo Consulting Group, Inc. International copyrights reserved in all countries.
No part of this book may be reproduced in any form without written permission from the publisher.
ABDO & Daughters™ is a trademark and logo of ABDO Publishing Company.

Printed in the United States.

Editor: Paul Joseph
Graphic Design: John Hamilton
Cover Design: Neil Klinepier
Cover Photo: Corbis
Interior Photos and Illustrations: AP/Wide World Photos, p. 3, 4, 5, 11, 13, 25, 27
    Corbis, p. 1, 6, 7, 8, 9, 12, 15, 17, 19, 20, 21, 24, 25, 28-29
    NOAA, p. 14, 16
    Digital Globe, p. 23
    John Hamilton, p. 22

Library of Congress Cataloging-in-Publication Data

Hamilton, John, 1959–
    Tsunamis / John Hamilton.
      p. cm. — (Nature's fury)
      Includes index.
    ISBN 1-59679-333-3
    1. Tsunamis—Juvenile literature. I. Title.

    GC221.5.H36 2006
    551.46'37—dc22

                        2005040427

CONTENTS

A survivor holds up a missing woman's portrait, which he retrieved from the rubble of Banda Aceh, Indonesia, after the devastating tsunami of December 26, 2004.

KILLER WAVE

FOR MANY PEOPLE IN SOUTH ASIA, THE SEA IS A BRINGER OF LIFE and livelihood. Coastal towns in countries like Indonesia, Sri Lanka, Thailand, and India depend on the sea for fishing, shipping, and tourism. It has always provided, giving generations of people reason to live. But on the morning of December 26, 2004, the sea brought death and destruction.

At approximately 7:59 a.m. local time, the earth trembled deep under the Indian Ocean off the coast of Sumatra, a province of Indonesia. The result was a magnitude 9.3 earthquake on the Richter scale, the second strongest ever recorded. A 750-mile (1,207-km) stretch of ocean floor ruptured, disturbing millions of tons of seawater. A tsunami (soo-NAH-mee), one of Earth's deadliest natural forces, was unleashed. The monster waves hurtled across the ocean at jetliner speed, devouring anything in their path.

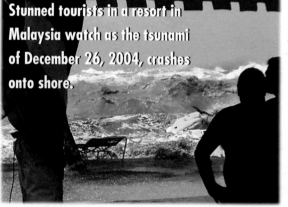

Stunned tourists in a resort in Malaysia watch as the tsunami of December 26, 2004, crashes onto shore.

Most people never saw it coming. There was very little official warning. The Pacific Ocean, which sees many tsunamis, has an electronic alert system that uses satellites and seismic sensors to warn people of impending waves. But a killer tsunami hadn't occurred in the Indian Ocean for hundreds of years. The countries bordering the ocean didn't think they were vulnerable to tsunamis. An early warning system, they believed, was not worth the millions of dollars it would have cost.

A U.S. Navy officer looks at the tsunami-devastated coast of Aceh from his Navy helicopter during emergency relief operations near Loh Kruet, 45 miles (72 km) southwest of Banda Aceh, Indonesia, January 11, 2005.

This video image shows the tsunami crashing over a sea wall in Penang, Malaysia.

At the Pacific Tsunami Warning Center, which is located in Hawaii, scientists using seismometers detected the earthquake in the Indian Ocean. At first they thought it was a magnitude 8.0 earthquake, very strong but not always catastrophic. As more data came in, the scientists realized the true power of the earthquake. An official warning was sent out: "There is a possibility of a tsunami near the epicenter." But by then it was too late for many people, and besides, there was no central system in place to warn the public in that part of the world.

Many people on the beaches that morning, including fishermen, tourists, or just plain passersby, noticed something strange about the ocean. The water pulled back, receding much farther than normal, even for a low tide. Some people thought it was because of the full moon. In fact, receding waters are one strong warning sign of an impending tsunami. But many people

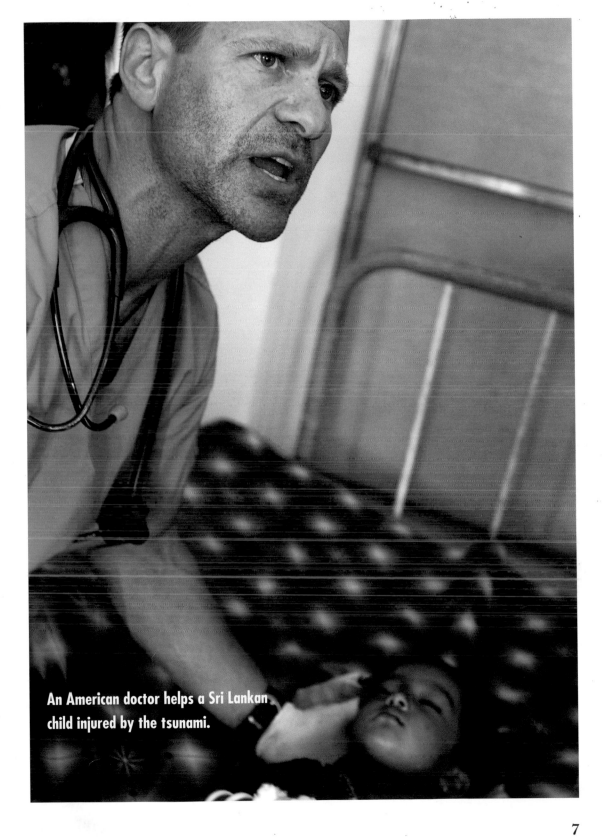

An American doctor helps a Sri Lankan child injured by the tsunami.

don't know about this, certainly not the droves of delighted children who combed the beaches picking up colorful fish that had been stranded by the rapid pulling back of the water.

An Indonesian soldier carries an injured woman to an emergency evacuation center.

And then, catastrophe struck. People heard what many described as a very loud roaring noise, like a jet airplane or train locomotive. Looking out to sea, people watched as an ominous wall of water rapidly approached the shore. Tsunamis don't usually look like the mountainous waves shown in Hollywood movies like *The Day After Tomorrow*.

Instead, this was a surge of brown-colored water that rose 30 feet (9.1 m) or more, high enough to crash onto shore and inundate coastal towns. Many people stood there on the beaches, transfixed, unable to move, while others fled in panic.

First to be hit were coastal villages on the remote northwestern end of Sumatra, nearest to the epicenter of the earthquake. The tsunami struck like a fist from the sea, brushing aside everything in its path. Buildings were crushed, cars swept aside like toys, trees and light poles snapped in two as if they were twigs. People by the thousands were caught up in the flood. Many were drowned, or killed when they were struck by debris. And the water kept coming, rushing inland for miles in some places, like a giant reaching in and killing without remorse or mercy.

Many places were struck by several waves, each of them bringing death and destruction. It often took the water hours to recede. When the terrible floods finally retreated back to the sea, whole communities were gone, wiped clean off the face of the earth.

After ravaging Sumatra, the waves spread out, moving rapidly across the open ocean. Thailand was struck next, with coastal villages and tourist resort beaches hit hardest. Burma and Bangladesh were next. Two hours after the earthquake, Sri Lanka and India felt the wrath of the waves. Hours later and thousands of miles away across the Indian Ocean, the still-potent tsunami struck the northeast coast of Africa, killing unsuspecting people in Somalia, Kenya, and Tanzania.

By the time it was over, more than 220,000 people had lost their lives to the killer waves (almost four times the number of people that fit inside New York City's Yankee Stadium), with many thousands more still missing and presumed dead. Tens of thousands of people were seriously injured. Millions were left destitute, with no homes or businesses to return to. It was one of the worst natural disasters in history.

An Indian woman mourns the death of her relative killed by the tsunami in Cuddalore, India.

THE SCIENCE OF TSUNAMIS

MANY PEOPLE SAY "TIDAL WAVE" TO DESCRIBE A DESTRUCTIVE wall of water, but that is not an accurate term. Tides are the natural rising and lowering of ocean levels at the shore caused by the gravitational pull of the moon. We know today that these waves are formed by the violent actions of the earth.

Almost all scientists today use the term "sea-wave," or the Japanese word "tsunami," which translates as "harbor wave." Tides have nothing to do with creating tsunamis. When tides are high, however, the severity of tsunamis is often increased.

Tsunamis occur when the ocean is disturbed. Scientists say that the seawater is "displaced" by an "impulsive disturbance." That just means that something big and powerful is moving a lot of water very quickly. Earthquakes are the most common source of tsunamis. Volcanic eruptions and underwater landslides are other common causes. Impact from outer space objects, such as asteroids, and underwater nuclear explosions can also cause tsunamis, although they are very rare.

The 2004 south Asia tsunami was caused by an earthquake. Normally, in that part of the world, two plates of the earth's crust, the Burma plate and the Indian plate, slowly grind against each other. The Indian plate pulls down on the Burma plate about 2.4 inches (6.1 cm) each year. On December 26, 2004, built-up stress caused a 750-mile (1,207 km) section of the Burma plate to snap upward like a giant paddle, displacing trillions of gallons of water and forcing it to move upward.

Once these gigantic masses of water surge to the surface, they spread outward in waves, which oftentimes

Deadly Walls of Water

Tsunamis travel very fast on the open ocean, but their destructive power comes from the towering heights they attain as they approach the coast. When they

strike, tsunamis can sweep away everything in their path. The photo at left is amateur video footage taken by a British tourist on December 26, 2004, from a hotel room in Beruwela, southwest Sri Lanka, at the moment the massive tsunami struck the beach-side vacation resort.

Seismic event or displacement sends shock waves outward.

As the depths get more shallow, the waves decrease in speed while increasing in height.

Initial waves travel very fast, but are only a few feet in height.

Waves travel through shallower depths as they approach the coast.

Tsunami waves hit shores with deadly force, depositing water and debris.

Sea level

Source: USGS/AP

cause massive destruction when they reach land. In the open ocean, however, tsunamis are stealthy. Waves that can hold the same energy as several nuclear bombs might cause barely a small swell in deep water.

Tsunamis in deep water might measure less than three feet (.9 m) tall, but they can reach lengths of 100 miles (161 km) or more from crest to crest. This makes tsunamis very difficult to spot in the open ocean. A tsunami might pass under a ship and never be noticed. And they move very fast, reaching speeds up to 500 miles per hour (805 km/hr), about the same speed as a jet airplane. They can move from one side of the Pacific Ocean to the other side in less than one day.

Lituya Bay, Alaska

As a tsunami gets closer to the coast, two things happen. As the wave travels over shallower water, it slows down, but without losing much energy. Also, the height of the wave grows. This is called a "shoaling" effect.

When tsunamis reach the shore, they sometimes appear as a rapidly rising tide, or a series of large breaking waves. The most violent tsunamis, which happen when the wave goes from deep water to a shallow bay or river, appear as frightening "bores." Bores are step-like walls of water. Tsunamis that crash into shore close to the epicenter of an earthquake can reach heights of 100 feet (30 m) or more. Oftentimes the water near shore retreats before the big waves hit, which is what happened in the south Asia tsunami.

In 1958, an earthquake registering 8.0 on the Richter scale shook Lituya Bay, in southeastern Alaska. The quake caused part of a mountain to slide into the water, spawning a tsunami that raced throughout the bay. When the wave reached the opposite bay shore, it produced a water surge measuring 1,722 feet (525 m), the largest local tsunami ever recorded. Trees and other vegetation, as well as any animals caught in the wave's path, were stripped clean off the mountain, leaving an ugly scar that still shows today. Two boaters on the bay at the time were killed, but several others miraculously survived.

The Source of Earthquakes

The earthquake that spawned the tsunami of December 26, 2004, originated in a fault dividing two plates of the earth's crust, the Burma plate and the Indian plate. When one side of a fault slips, it causes an earthquake which then could cause a tsunami.

Types of plate boundaries

Transform
Two plates sliding along each other.

Divergent
Two plates are slowly moving away from each other.

Convergent

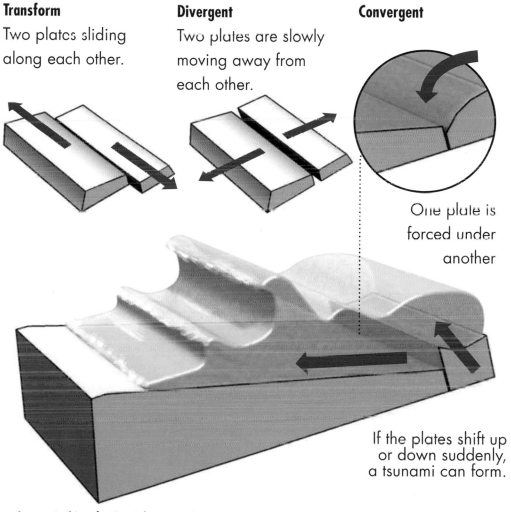

One plate is forced under another

If the plates shift up or down suddenly, a tsunami can form.

Source: Int'l Inst. for Geo-Information Science and Earth Observation/AP

HILO, HAWAII

BECAUSE THE STATE OF HAWAII IS IN THE MIDDLE OF THE Pacific Ocean, it is often affected by devastating tsunamis. On May 22, 1960, a magnitude 9.5 earthquake occurred off the coast of Chile, South America. It was the largest earthquake ever recorded, and spawned a series of deadly waves that quickly spread across the Pacific Ocean basin.

Less than 15 minutes after the quake, walls of water killed thousands of people along the coast of Chile. Fifteen hours later, the tsunami reached the Hawaiian islands. The city of Hilo, on the island of Hawaii, was hardest hit. The tsunami destroyed Hilo's waterfront area. Piers were wrecked, houses and

A man in the lower left of this photo watches helplessly as a tsunami engulfs the city of Hilo, Hawaii, on April 1, 1946.

businesses swept away, and parking meters bent in two. The tsunami killed 61 people in Hilo. After it moved on, it damaged coastal communities as far away as Japan.

It wasn't the first time Hilo had been battered by a tsunami. On April 1, 1946, a magnitude 7.8 earthquake pummeled Alaska's Aleutian Islands, creating a killer tsunami. Five hours later, with no warning, the waves had raced across the ocean and crashed into Hawaii. In Hilo, 159 people were killed. Much of the town was wiped out.

Because of the severity of this tsunami, in 1949 the United States established the Pacific Tsunami Warning Center in Hawaii, with the goal of tracking Pacific Ocean waves and alerting coastal communities of danger.

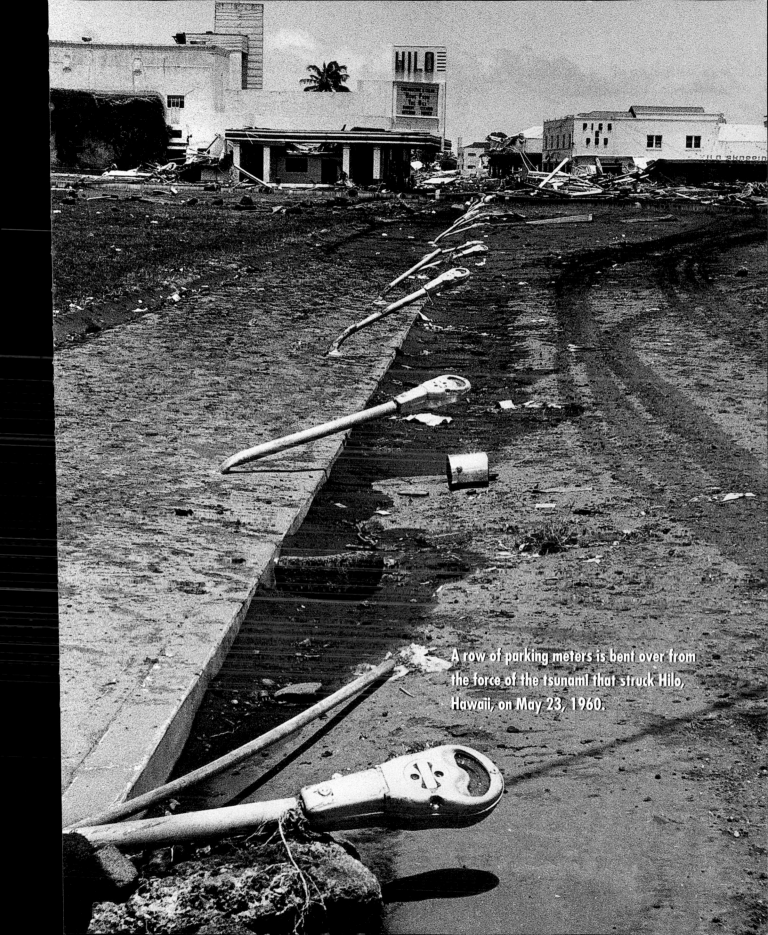

A row of parking meters is bent over from the force of the tsunami that struck Hilo, Hawaii, on May 23, 1960.

THE GREAT ALASKAN TSUNAMI

THE STRONGEST EARTHQUAKE EVER RECORDED IN NORTH America happened on March 27, 1964, in southern Alaska. The 9.2-magnitude earthquake was centered in northern Prince William Sound, about 75 miles (121 km) east of Anchorage, Alaska. The quake was felt in large parts of the state, as well as parts of western Yukon Territory and British Columbia, Canada.

In downtown Anchorage, the ground shook for a full five minutes. People were knocked off their feet, buildings collapsed, and landslides destroyed neighborhoods. Nine people were killed by the earthquake, but the worst was yet to come.

Under the sea, huge sections of the ocean floor were suddenly thrust upwards. The violent shaking also caused underwater landslides. The result was the most disastrous tsunami to ever hit the United States west coast and Canada's British Columbia. Many towns along the Gulf of Alaska were devastated. At the Valdez Inlet, the wave reached a height of 220 feet (67 m), scouring everything in its path.

Wreckage strewn on the shore of Seward, Alaska.

The shoreline of Valdez, Alaska, was devastated by the 1964 tsunami.

The tsunami killed 106 people in Alaska. It then raced southward at 500 miles per hour (805 km/hr), slamming into coastal communities in Canada and the west coast of the United States. In Oregon, four young campers on a beach were swept away and killed. And in Crescent City, California, a 21-foot (6.4-m) wave washed out roads and bridges and destroyed hundreds of homes and businesses. Eleven people were killed.

KRAKATOA

DURING THE LAST 250 YEARS, THERE WERE APPROXIMATELY 90 tsunamis that were caused by volcanoes alone. Of those, the biggest and most destructive of all was the 1883 eruption of Krakatoa in southeast Asia. Krakatoa is a volcano on the Indonesian island of Rakata, which lies between Java and Sumatra in the Sunda Strait.

When Krakatoa erupted, the sound of the explosion was heard as far away as Australia, 2,200 miles (3,500 km) away. On Rodriguez Island, 2,968 miles (4,776 km) away in the Indian Ocean, a police chief clearly heard the sound, mistaking it for naval gunfire.

Krakatoa's eruption sent a tower of fiery ash into the sky nearly 30 miles (48 km) high. Most of the island was obliterated. Ash and debris darkened the local sky, and day became night. Volcanic dust affected world temperatures for many months after the eruption.

The Dutch ship Berouw is washed away by a tsunami created by the eruption.

Because Krakatoa is in such a remote location, there were relatively few deaths due just to the explosion. However, the eruption spawned a series of four immensely fast and tall tsunamis that spread outward, which caused horrible destruction in the region. Some waves reached heights of 131 feet (40 m), obliterating everything in their path.

The shores of Java and Sumatra were smashed. Black walls of water wiped 165 villages out of existence. The giant waves killed nearly 40,000 people. The bodies of victims were found in the ocean for weeks after the eruption.

Today, the smoldering remains of Krakatoa continues to rumble and belch smoke. The volcano has risen, growing taller at a rate of about five inches (12.7 cm) per week. No one knows when Krakatoa will erupt again, but most geologists agree that it is only a matter of time.

When Krakatoa erupted in 1883, the sound was so great that it was heard thousands of miles away. The resulting tsunamis killed tens of thousands of people in southeast Asia.

CALAMITY IN SOUTH ASIA

THE TSUNAMI OF DECEMBER 26, 2004, BROUGHT UNIMAGINABLE misery to the people of south Asia. By the time the killer waves had receded, more than 220,000 people had lost their lives, with many tens of thousands more missing and presumed dead.

By far the hardest hit was the northwestern tip of the Indonesian island of Sumatra. The epicenter of the earthquake that caused the tsunami was just offshore. More than 70 percent of the people in some coastal villages were killed by the wall of water that slammed into the coast. One month after the tsunami struck, the Indonesian government reported more than 95,000 of its citizens had been buried, and another 133,000 were missing and presumed dead. The exact number of dead may never be known. More than 800,000 people were left homeless. Countless people lost their jobs and businesses.

A Sri Lankan teenager wears a shirt over his mouth to help mask the stench of rotting bodies.

More than 100 aid groups, including the United Nations, began helping in Indonesia. The military forces of 11 nations, with the United States leading the way, were sent to the region to help with disaster relief efforts. Many

A mosque is the only building left standing in a village on the west coast of Aceh Province on the Indonesian island of Sumatra.

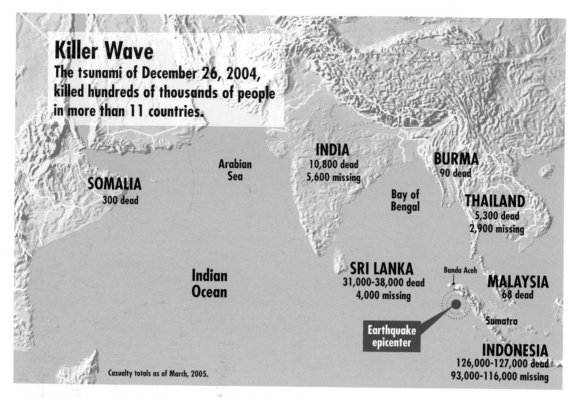

Killer Wave
The tsunami of December 26, 2004, killed hundreds of thousands of people in more than 11 countries.

SOMALIA
300 dead

Arabian Sea

INDIA
10,800 dead
5,600 missing

BURMA
90 dead

THAILAND
5,300 dead
2,900 missing

Bay of Bengal

Indian Ocean

SRI LANKA
31,000-38,000 dead
4,000 missing

Banda Aceh

MALAYSIA
68 dead

Earthquake epicenter

Sumatra

INDONESIA
126,000-127,000 dead
93,000-116,000 missing

Casualty totals as of March, 2005.

countries donated food, water, shelter, medicine, and money. People from all over the world made donations to help the victims. Billions of dollars were pledged.

Aircraft and ships brought in huge loads of relief supplies. These were then put on trucks, small planes, or helicopters to get aid where it was needed most. However, many bridges and harbors were washed away by the tsunami. Helicopters became very important in reaching many areas.

Two weeks after the tsunami, U.N. Secretary General Kofi Annan and U.S. Secretary of State Colin Powell toured the region. Both were shocked by the enormity of the disaster. In many places there was no sign of life, with destruction stretching as far as the eye could see. Annon said, "I have never seen such utter destruction mile after mile, and you wonder, 'where are the people? What happened to them?'"

Said Colin Powell in an interview with CNN, "No briefing book, no television picture can convey what really happened here."

After striking Indonesia, the killer waves radiated outward, slamming next

Satellite images of Banda Ache, Indonesia, taken before (top) and after (below) the tsunami struck on December 26, 2004.

A U.S. Seahawk helicopter from the U.S.S. Abraham Lincoln carrier group delivers desperately needed supplies to tsunami survivors in Indonesia.

into coastal villages in Malaysia and Thailand. The west coast of Thailand was severely damaged. At least 5,300 people were killed, many of them foreigners on vacation at popular resorts near the city of Phuket.

About two hours after the earthquake, the first wave sped across the Bay of Bengal and slammed into the island nation of Sri Lanka. At least 34,000 people were killed, with many thousands more missing. A staggering one million people were left homeless.

Next struck was the southeast coast of India. More than 8,800 people were killed, with thousands more missing and presumed dead. At least 140,000 Indians were left homeless.

Almost eight hours after the quake, the tsunami slammed into the east coast of Africa. Somalia was hardest hit. More than 200 people are thought to have been killed there.

The loss of life and the extent of damage from the south Asia tsunami are mind-boggling. It will take many years and many billions of dollars, but with the world's help, the struggling people of the region should someday be able to rebuild their lives.

A rescue crew (above) surveys a flooded hotel lobby on Phuket Island, Thailand. Boats lie stacked atop one another (below) in a harbor in India.

FUTURE DANGER

BECAUSE SCIENCE CAN'T YET PREDICT WHEN EARTHQUAKES will occur, they also can't tell when tsunamis will strike. However, using historical records and computer predictions, scientists can estimate fairly accurately where future tsunamis are likely to occur.

On average, there are two destructive tsunamis each year in the Pacific Ocean basin. Because of this, an early warning system has been set up to alert people along the coasts of incoming tsunamis.

The Pacific tsunami warning system consists of a series of buoys and underwater sensors that detect earthquakes and waves. Data is transmitted by satellite to scientists, who can then warn the public by radio, television, or warning sirens along the affected coastlines.

The destructive 2004 south Asia tsunami made countries realize that all vulnerable coastlines should have warning systems installed, despite their expense. This includes the Atlantic and Indian Ocean basins, which experience destructive tsunamis only rarely. The cost of doing nothing is too high when millions of lives are at stake. Besides taking advantage of early warning systems, coastal communities can help minimize the damage caused by tsunamis by building sturdy sea walls and planting vegetation, such as mangrove trees, in shallow waters near shore. The south Asia tsunami might not have hit some areas so hard, especially resort areas in Thailand, if protective vegetation hadn't been cleared away to make room for boat docks and beaches.

One area that worries many people is the island of La Palma, in the Canary Islands, just off the northwest coast

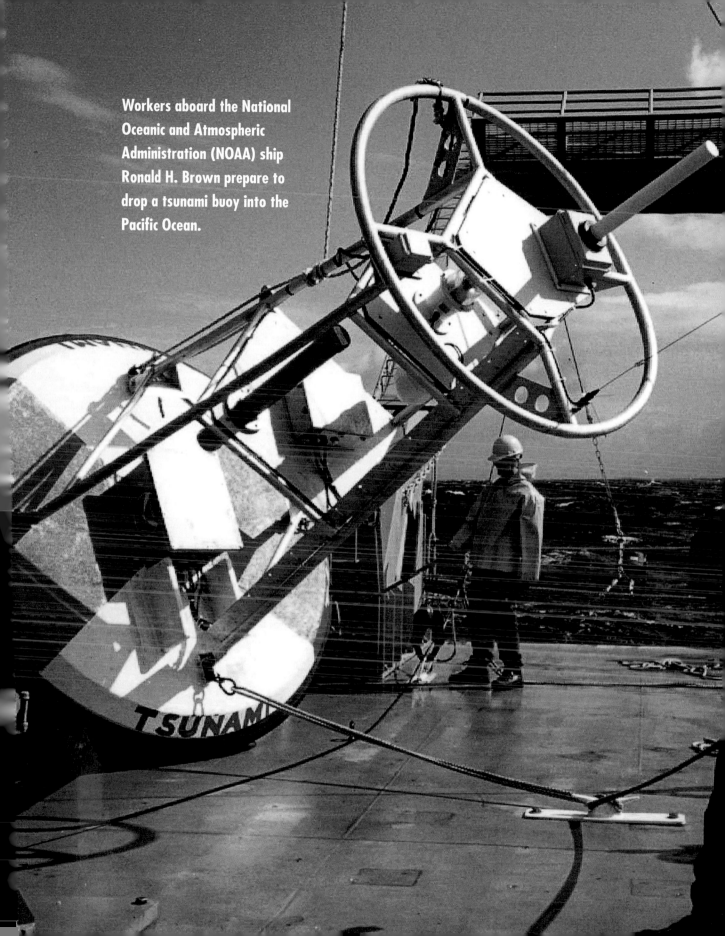

Workers aboard the National Oceanic and Atmospheric Administration (NOAA) ship Ronald H. Brown prepare to drop a tsunami buoy into the Pacific Ocean.

of Africa in the Atlantic Ocean. La Palma is volcanic, and scientists have detected a large fault line splitting the island. They worry that a future eruption or earthquake might cause a huge section of the island to fall into the sea, spawning a "mega tsunami" thousands of feet high that could race across the Atlantic Ocean and devastate coastal cities. Many scientists agree it will eventually happen, but they can't predict when. It might happen tomorrow, but more likely not for hundreds, possibly thousands, of years from now.

People continue to live in places where the risk for tsunamis is high. Coastal areas in Japan, the Philippines, even along the American west coast and Hawaii, are overdue for a tsunami. People are attracted to the beauty of mountainous coastlines, islands, and peninsulas, plus the moderate climate brought by ocean currents. Unfortunately, the most attractive areas that people choose to live are often the most vulnerable. The damage and loss of life that occurs when future tsunamis finally strike will depend on how prepared people are to meet nature's fury.

A tsunami survivor walks past huge fishing boats pushed onto the shore of Banda Aceh, Indonesia.

GLOSSARY

EPICENTER

The part of the earth's surface directly above the place of origin, or focus, of an earthquake.

PACIFIC TSUNAMI WARNING CENTER

Established in 1949, the Pacific Tsunami Warning Center in Ewa Beach, Hawaii, provides tsunami warnings to most countries in the Pacific Ocean basin as well as Hawaii and all other U.S. interests in the Pacific outside of Alaska and the U.S. west coast.

RICHTER SCALE

A scale used to measure the strength, or magnitude, of earthquakes. The Richter scale is a *logarithmic* scale: each step is about 10 times stronger than the one before it. For example, an earthquake measuring 7.0 on the Richter scale is ten times greater than an earthquake measuring 6.0. An earthquake measuring 1.0 on the Richter scale is so small it is detectable only by scientific instruments. An earthquake measuring 7.0 can cause major damage to buildings.

SEISMOMETER

A scientific instrument, also called a seismograph, which records the movements of the earth. Seismometers are used to detect earthquakes, and to measure their strength on the Richter scale.

SHOALING EFFECT

When a tsunami reaches shallow water near a coastline. The wave slows down and increases in height.

SUNDA STRAIT

A body of water between the islands of Java and Sumatra in the country of Indonesia. It connects the Java Sea to the Indian Ocean. It is an important route for shipping. There are several islands in the strait, including Rakata, on which rests Krakatoa, the volcano that exploded in 1883. The resulting tsunamis killed tens of thousands of people in south Asia.

TIDAL WAVE

Many people refer to tsunamis as tidal waves. This is not an accurate term, because tides have nothing to do with creating tsunamis. Tides are a raising or lowering of ocean levels caused by the gravitational pull of the moon. Tsunamis are caused by powerful forces under the ocean that suddenly displace massive amounts of water, which then cause large waves to spread out in all directions. Tsunamis are commonly triggered by earthquakes, volcanic eruptions, or underwater landslides.

WEB SITES

WWW.ABDOPUB.COM

Would you like to learn more about tsunamis? Please visit www.abdopub.com to find up-to-date Web site links about tsunamis and other natural disasters. These links are routinely monitored and updated to provide the most current information available.

INDEX